Seasons of Change

poems by

Ed Block

Finishing Line Press
Georgetown, Kentucky

Seasons of Change

Copyright © 2017 by Ed Block
ISBN 978-1-63534-365-6 First Edition
All rights reserved under International and Pan-American Copyright Conventions.
No part of this book may be reproduced in any manner whatsoever without written permission from the publisher, except in the case of brief quotations embodied in critical articles and reviews.

ACKNOWLEDGMENTS

The following poems have previously appeared as indicated:

"Crows" and "Spring Migration" in *Lake Country Journal*
"Looking for Norma," "From the Air," "Hotel Malawi," "Spring Flood," and "Peonies in Autumn" in *Literary Matters*

Publisher: Leah Maines

Editor: Christen Kincaid

Cover Art: Ed Block

Author Photo: Ed Block

Cover Design: Elizabeth Maines McCleavy

Printed in the USA on acid-free paper.
Order online: www.finishinglinepress.com
        also available on amazon.com

Author inquiries and mail orders:
Finishing Line Press
P. O. Box 1626
Georgetown, Kentucky 40324
U. S. A.

Table of Contents

My Readers
At Home
A Spring Migration 1
Spring Flood 2
Morning in the Country 3
My Ladder 4
In Africa
Hotel Malawi 5
Late Night at Mwale's 6
Chikale Beach 7
Cinzano White, and Red 8
Back Home
At an Exhibition 9
Casida 10
Zen in Walnut Creek 11
Rummage Sale 12
Red-Spotted Purple 13
35th and Morgan 14
Suburban Derelict 15
Before Midnight 16
Looking for Norma 17
September Song 18
Peonies in Fall 19
Autumn Nocturne 20
October Farewell 21
The Crows 22
Their Mortal Lives 23

In Florida
A Map 24
In the Keys with Maggie 25
On Key West 26
Duval Street 27

Back Home Again
Tam's Gone Dark 28
From the Air 29
After Snowfall 30

My Readers

You're like a whiff of perfume,
or is it smoke
from a cigar? You sit there
in the corner, in the dark.

On the way to work,
a macchiato. As you wait,
you turn the pages of a magazine
and find me there.

You meet this poem at the loneliest
moment of the day, cold cup
of coffee in your hand.
You turn the page
and there I am.

At home, you smile at lines
that make you think
I know what you
are thinking;
then you frown.
He doesn't know at all.

You turn the page but half-remember
something that I said. It makes you
smile again; your smile is happy,
peaceful, radiant to behold.
                                  Your husband
enters, sees you smiling; asks,
"What's that you're smiling at?"
You say, "It's nothing; only
something I just read."

AT HOME

A Spring Migration
>   *for Ted Kooser*

The snow around the tree recedes.
Their winter trails exposed, the voles
make for the matted leaves, the cracks
between the Lannon stone;

the gaps beneath the bent and broken iris stems
that mark the garden's edge. They
curse the march of spring and vow
to stay abed all day, when once
they find their summer home again.

Spring Flood
    (Aldo's Carp)

In the rows
now flooded by the river,
carp swim happily.

They wriggle through
the drowned cornstalks,
rubbing scaly sides
against the green,
and whisper to each other.

Spring explorers, these,
they kiss the mud
with baby mouths.

But, interlopers, they churn
up the water, finding
leaves and cobs left
from the fall.

Till water recedes,
the carp intrude
in foreign territories,
making fun
of patient farmers' plows.

Morning in the Country

The sun's up, clouds
cling to his jeans. He dusts
them off, mist settles in the hollows.
He plods across the field, boots
leaving shadows in the glades.
He heads uphill to farms where birds
he'd freed last night call out
for breakfast. Scatters corn
like gold, then rubs his palms with light.

My Ladder

Against the wall
beside the door
inside the dark garage
my ladder leans;
at twenty-four,
the oldest tool in this
our second house.
The dabs of brown and cream
that spatter steps and rails
recall our coming here.
The ladder knows more
than it's telling
of lives, our climbs,
descents, and shaky
standing still. The ladder,
upright, in its proper place,
is way too smart
to judge.

IN AFRICA

Hotel Malawi
    Homage to Charles Simic

I liked my digs, a window on the jungle.
At dusk, the monkeys stared at me.
Outside, the villagers walked
down the clay path, through the *dambo*
to the tea plantation. A crippled woman
carried a suitcase on her head.

Mostly, though, I sought the quiet after dark;
the rooms, with spiders, fleas and roaches
that wore brown jackets, underneath the iron bed;
the geckos dreaming on the walls; a night so black
I scarcely looked outside, lest horrors
meet me in the windows' mirror.

At 5 A.M. the voices in the dawn,
the bare feet soughing in the dark—
imagined women, Dar-cloth skirts,
baskets on their heads. Going to the john—
another night of too much native beer—I heard
a baby's cry; pictured it tightly wrapped
on mother's back, and thought
I heard a months old homesick cry.

Late Night at Mwale's

A dark September night,
a smoky native bar
with grimy concrete steps;
its thatched roof reeking paraffin.

The volunteers, their classes
out, have biked
along the gravel roads
beneath the dust-green trees
that line the village street.

The Bantu barmaid wears
a Dar-cloth *saru*, a bright
bandana on her head. She smiles
with one tooth gone in front.

The regulars: a lorry driver
in from Blantyre, farmers
and three clerks in soiled white shirts.

The young white men
will drink and sing
until the morning light,
then mount their Honda 90's
once again and drive home,
weaving through the misty bush
and toward a tryst with dawn.

Chikale Beach

Down to the bay
in the gathering dusk,
then out through town.
Beyond the DC's house
and shadows loom ahead.

The bridge across the *dambo*,
rotted, scarce will hold
the load of motorcycle,
man—and woman
clinging to his back,
like a cricket
to its mate.

Uphill and then
a dusty, steep
descent into the crowd
that gathers at the beach.

On the sloping sand
they've lit a fire.
There they dance,
drink Carlsberg beer
or Malawi Gin and lime
until the morning haze
arises like an Ngoni warrior.

Then they mount their rides
again, escape through jungle
towards a sunrise over Africa.

Cinzano White, and Red

A gaudy restaurant poster for vermouth;
the grapes, the swirls of color, edged
in black, around a supine model
whose flying hair obscures her face.

The flavor of the sight is sweet, astringent,
with just a hint of wormwood;
passion over ice, enjoyed
before and after meals
or sex.

Years ago, it was a favorite
drink in Central Africa.

Pungent midnight, the southern stars so near;
ex-pat passengers, female and male;
lovers and friends on the open upper deck;
a packet, anchored in the bay.

Faint lights from the shore, reflected on the water,
mix with the stars. Below,
the sounds of Bantu passengers
embarking noisily; the thrumming
of the diesel, surging, surging to push off.

Now the present takes possession
of the past again. But the past
refuses to dissolve.

A ship sets out for Mozambique, the north;
a steamy Greene adventure, freighted
with passion and regrets.

So now, a farewell sip,
a final toast. You ghosts
of yesteryear, adieu.
Return, remain; so far
away, so near, so dear.

BACK HOME

At an Exhibition

A shapely blonde—in partial profile, sleeveless
black shell, patterned skirt—looks sidelong
at a life-size Art Nouveau, an odalisque
in striking black and white, who, like a wanton,
breasts and cleft exposed, long legs
extended leisurely, against a *Judgendstil*
background, reclines, a Klimt-inspired robe
snaking about her curves. She lounges
on a pillow, face shaped by short hair
that frames an eyeless space, the lips and nipples
poised expressive of a cool eroticism.

Casida
after Federico Garcia Lorca

To see you nude is to see the truth
the smooth truth, clear of cats.
The truth without a bloom, a naked shape
forgetful of the past, a place of coal.

To see you nude is to know desire
like lightning that would break forth
or the self-devouring sea, whose maw
cannot but swallow all it meets.

My bile will surge through bedrooms
and descend with unsheathed blade
but you will ignore the army
and its fragile flower power,

your mons, a prize to scale,
your mouth a hazy evening.
Under your spreading branches
prior lovers moan, remembering you.

Zen in Walnut Creek
for Tom and Mary

I fell asleep in total dark,
but wake to eerie light.
Through the wood blinds
the night sky turns from
black, to blue-black—
then – to blue-gray, heralding the dawn.

A waning moon
and one bright star—
beneath and to the left—
seem motionless in space.

Unearthly brilliance streams
between the blinds.
Outside the window, to one side,
 a single juniper—in silhouette—
completes what now appears
an Oriental scene.

Rummage Sale

An ordinary August Saturday. Then,
in the neighborhood, a kind of magic;
old faces stare from older picture frames;
sterling silver, plant arrangements, canning jars,

an antique lamp, old books,
a box of dated record albums,
painted birdhouses, a baize card table, dishes,
make-up mirrors, a German choir book.

The visitors drawn slowly up the driveway
in the sun, threading the narrow aisles,
stop to peer at hand-sewn toys, or turn
a porcelain elephant in their hands.

Swept into the dark garage itself,
in rusty light, damp carpet
beneath low rafters, here they try
on funny glasses by the light of a dirty bulb.

Past chipped, enameled pans and faux
Depression glass, to Rosie, eighty years old,
lurking behind the tables in an easy
chair, the darkest corner of the room.

A spider in her web, she weaves her words;
the past hangs in her hair like dust. Outside
the sun shines off the asphalt drive, and buyers,
blinded, emerge with cobwebs in their heads.

Red-Spotted Purple

Uncommon name, a common
Midwest butterfly; find it
on the roadsides, in the road.
It poises lightly on the muddy
ground. It also lands on dung.

May to October one can come
as a surprise; a spot of blue that interrupts
a walk. Cold-blooded, like a snake,
it basks in the sun, wings open, veins
conveying heat along the filmy membranes.

Brush-footed, tarsi-tasting flowers; its dark
wings, covered with fine dusty scales,
have an iridescent hue. The feet,
with little claws, help grip the leaves.

A look-alike for its toxic cousin:
the red-orange spots can be most stunning.
With opening and closing of its wings,
it gives a sense of peace and new beginnings.

35th & Morgan

A house atop a hill,
garage door half collapsed,
a slanted porch above;
in front an unkempt lawn.

The duplex window shades
pulled down unevenly,
the front door open wide
this cold November morning.

To see straight through the hall
into a living room
and dining room feels
almost obscene—

a woman, legs spread wide,
and lying on her back.

Suburban Derelict

A cluttered porch, forgotten
and unvisited, its awning coated
by neglect, the badly painted door a ruin.

The eaves drip desolation,
the sidewalk strewn with leaves
of loss. The driveway cratered

by the cares of decades. Flowerbeds
are weed-choked with forgetfulness.
The empty mailbox gapes decrepitude.

Around the corner, more suburban slums;
a sign "For Rent" obscured by buckthorn, toys
abandoned on the street, a kite upended in a tree.

Before Midnight

The dark street stands deserted.
Only the home, emptied
by divorce, with one dim bulb,

glows weakly, like a dying body.
Its cone of light surveys the yard—
a garden overgrown and haunted

by ghosts of parties past;
a phantom swimming pool
where only shadows float.

The shrouded moon emerges,
an aged Charon counting
small change into a trembling hand.

Looking for Norma

After decades, I've been looking for you, Norma,
in the basement of my heart. The light from boarded windows,
bad, the lamps without their bulbs.

The furnace now is old, the plumbing on the verge.
The empty bar is dry, the table tennis table piled
with junk and extra mattresses. Absurd!

I moved the boxes, caught in cobwebs, re-arranged
the toys. I opened musty trunks of memories. I felt
the pulse of days forgotten; found a battered dress,

some yellow underwear; old hats and model airplanes.
Pictures in old frames stare back at me. I read the books and
poems you gave me, tried on clothes
that you once wore.

I lay upon the broken couch, its springs poked
through my back. Beneath the workbench, dust
and mouse turds stopped my search.
I crawled back up the stairs and poured a drink
before I called the hearse.

September Song

The porch stands empty as the air turns cold.
The cushions on the chairs, unused for weeks,
seem faded from neglect. On either side the rails:
catoneasters and cone flowers droop,
and daddy long-legs cease their summer dance.
The cobwebs in the trellis hang in tatters,
bumble bees fly slowly to their graves.
The wasps are all asleep in paper tunnels
under-eave. The chipmunk families
have all left town.   The water in the barrel
now reflects the aging moon.
Only the cricket plays encores
of his sad September tune.

Peonies in Fall

In autumn, after cold September rains
have browned their beds, the peonies
are left alone, leaves tarnished,
stalks now thin as spinsters' legs.
They hang over their metal rings
in tangles, seeking anyone to hold them up.

All fertile fullness gone, their seed pods –
shriveled vulvas of old maids –
exposed to cold October winds; their fancy
dresses from June a distant memory
of pink and white.

                        With bees
and other suitors gone, the flowerbed
becomes a home for ghosts and other haunts—
the summer's last cicadas hidden there,
and spiders in their tattered webs,
too cold to move beyond their vortices.

Autumn Nocturne

The smell of burning leaves, the end
of summer. V's of geese leave the empty
skies, and cold thoughts gather as the moths
grow fewer, languid, and more leaves
fall from the trees. A pennyful of rain
disturbs the peace. On the porch the oil lamp's flame
becomes a dancer on the verge of night.
The wind chime quiets after dark; a single bird
echoes in the hedge. The time elapsed
is longer than the time ahead.

Cicadas weave a wickerwork of longing
in the tangled weeds that edge the dormant yard.
Smoke drifts lake-ward, drawn by the night wind
yearning homeward. Footsteps echo
out of sight along the sidewalk. Now
this only night the breeze has stilled.
The purling fountain, at the full,
consoles the mind; says: find some peace
in merely listening, in being wholly here.

October Farewell

The air is cold; the sky
portends a change of weather.
Leaves are falling on the lawn.
The garden's done at last,
the patio is empty
of the furniture and pots
that brightened the yard the summer long.

And now the cricket, like an old man,
stiff with cold, slowly crosses
the picnic table, longing for a bed.
It raises one thin leg and then another,
reaches out a feeler, like a cane,
then pauses, tests the air,
and knows its time has come to leave.

Crows

The crows,
like broken pieces
of the night,
dance out
above the roofs
and swirl
among the treetops
and the yards.

Late afternoon
and dingy concrete
of a broken road,
lead me to think
of crows
as harbingers of fall.

Their Mortal Lives
Homage to Ted Kooser

Today my birds peck red and yellow seeds
that scatter from the frozen feeder.
They scuff the seeds around; six sparrows
puffed up against the cold.
Like homeless hobos rummaging
the trash, they push
their beaks into the icy piles.

Nothing escapes them.
Cars on the street, a movement
on the sidewalk spooks them;
sends them diving into the junipers,
then, just as fast, they're back
and chowing down.

The temperature will drop tonight,
another wind-chill warning posted.
The birds, oblivious to weathermen,
thermometers, and forecasts;
will feel it, though, throughout
a long black night.

In the morning I'll fill
the empty feeder, and once again
the birds will come, or not.

What hot resolve burns
in those feathered breasts?
How many die
before the blue bowl
of the morning sky returns?

IN FLORIDA

A Map

A great sea turtle swims
across the map, its mottled
shell and fins an iridescent
hue with flashes,
green, orange and blue.
Beneath the turtle, Tarpon Bay,
Captiva Island swim,
complete with roads and bridges.
Follow the shore to Knapps Point,
out, then round the island to the causeway.

A keen observer hears
the waves beat on the southern
shore. The detailed markings
conjure visions of shells
and sand and crowded
thoroughfares. Depth markings
in the Gulf will cool the heat
along the Periwinkle Way.
But still the map at best implies
the vastness stretching south
and west, with shrimp boats rolling
in the swells, the dolphins diving,
and mirages that are Naples' towers
far, far out, just at the verge of visible.

In the Keys with Maggie
(Homage to Elizabeth Bishop)

My place on Summerland,
        my prince's palace,
cozy as a clam; it's vinyl and aluminum
        a double-wide,
with A/C on the roof, a picture
        window on the sea.

This dump, my love-nest,
        sports bleached oak
for cabinets, a cast-
        iron fry pan in a stainless
tub. The laundry hangs
        outside; my girl-
friend, Maggie's bra and panties
        next to oilskins
that I wear
        when I go fishing
in the Gulf, for tarpon,
        oysters, razorbacks,
which seldom bite.

When I come home,
        we drink tequila,
jump in bed
        and don't wake up
until the morning light
        when we hear roosters
crow, or tourists
        on the causeway.
And better than the fish,
        my Maggie bites.

On Key West

The pier, infatuated by the ocean
steps out boldly on her long
thin legs. The gaps between
her skinny boards reveal
the seething tide.
The waves caress her legs
as she reaches out, so tall,
so lonely, toward the gray horizon,
smiling cynically.

The cold excites, the foam arouses;
shadows play around the eddies
and the vortices that make
her see her future in a mating
with a giant wave that strips her,
leaves her standing naked
beneath the swirling sky.
Accused of carelessness and pride,
she is a creature of the land,
too eager for the depth that fools
us all by seeming what we most desire.

Duval Street

Down Duval, swept with the crowd
of visitors, to the shore. The cruise
ship towers over everything: the tourist trains,
the pirates, and the pretty maids
with tattooed legs and arms
who walk along, tall drinks above their heads.
The pedicabs joust with the motorbikes.
Street artists swim against the waves
of men in shorts and women in straw hats,
and sandals, swirling skirts. Expensive cars
display their chrome and tinted glass
and push through crowded streets.
But in the byways, beneath live oaks
and bougainvillea, the shadows gather.
Roosters scratch and root beneath the duff,
under the slash pines and the cypresses,
as if in search of keys to mysteries.
A breeze from off the Gulf portends
a storm before nightfall. The drunken
chef shouts from the back door
of the Commodore, wishing himself
back in the days of Henry Flagler
or Ernest Hemingway, dark ghosts
who gather over the Dry Tortugas,
red sundown a heartbeat's length away.

BACK HOME AGAIN

Tam's Gone Dark

Snow lies deep in the parking lot
of the Chinese restaurant. Closed.
Abandoned? No deliveries? No
late-night carry-outs, with soy
sauce in the little plastic bags?
No Egg foo Yung? The sign,
"Chop Suey," hangs at an angle,
as it had for years before
this sudden end. No boiling
oil in woks? no paper hats,
black aprons, or black slippers
on the help? The Chinese lanterns
above the door are dark; two snow-white
plaster lions crouch beside the entrance,
guarding the place from no one, now.

From the Air

Above the plane, immensity;
below, a winter desert,
lit in places.
Millions sleep beneath
the billions of cold lights—

like snowflakes
frozen in a void – while one,
a sleepless father
turns on a porch light
for an errant daughter,
drawn by phantom novas
from the bright way
leading home.

After Snowfall

The snow comes from the west;
the suburbs feel it first.
It drifts down quietly,
like syllables at dusk.
The snow is softly spoken.

At dawn the world, transformed,
appears illumined in its simple shapes
and monochrome. The inner life of cities—
tracks that we forget or fail to pay attention to—
snow re-presents to us, a gift
for recollectedness.

As words emplot and order,
snow transforms pursuit to pattern.
The cat beneath the fence
stands suddenly
beside the mouse
whose tracks lead willy-nilly to its hole.

The unseen birds,
whose songs have
brightened winter's filth,
are present, now,
around the garbage can, designing
their desires upon the covered
ground and in the drifted feeder overhead.

Ed Block was born in Manitowoc, Wisconsin. His father worked field construction throughout the American West in the 1950s and early 60s. The family settled in St. Paul, Minnesota where he attended Nazareth Hall high school and then St. Thomas College. After a year of graduate school at Stanford University on a Woodrow Wilson Fellowship, he spent two years in Malawi, Central Africa as a Peace Corps Volunteer teaching at a boarding secondary school near Nkhata Bay. He met his future wife, a lay mission volunteer, when she visited Chikale Beach, a cove just south of Nkhata Bay.

On his return to the U.S., he completed his Ph.D. in English and comparative literature at Stanford, married Mary Helen McLaren, and after a year in Germany on a Fulbright Fellowship, and two years teaching at Oregon State University, he accepted a tenure-track position at Marquette University, where he taught for thirty-five years. He and his wife raised three talented girls to womanhood. He retired from Marquette as Emeritus Professor in 2012.

He began publishing poetry in 1997 with a poem in *CrossCurrents*. Since then he has published over fifty poems in journals like *Spiritus, Review for Religious, Janus Head, Parabola, Nebraska Life,* and *Lake Country Journal*. In 2016 he published a collection of religious poems, *Anno Domini*. He was interviewed on a local religious radio station and Milwaukee's NPR show, "Lake Effect."

His reviews, interviews, and essays on literary topics and attentiveness in everyday life have appeared in *America, Image, Commonweal, Logos, U.S. Catholic,* and a variety of other journals. He continues to write poems and essays, tend a garden, and enjoy retirement in Greendale, Wisconsin.

www.ingramcontent.com/pod-product-compliance
Lightning Source LLC
LaVergne TN
LVHW041508070426
835507LV00012B/1410